Two Cups of Tomatoes

A Collection of Poems

by

Janelle Rainer

Two Cups of Tomatoes

© Janelle Rainer, 2015

Published by agreement with
PunksWritePoemsPress LLC
Chesterfield, VA

Catalog #: PWP003

ISBN: 0986170720

ISBN 13: 978-0-9861707-2-0

Cover painting by Janelle Rainer.

www.punkswritepoems.com

Table of Contents

I.

His Yelling   9
August, Age 24   10
Blame   11
Unguarded   14
Honey, I'm Home   15
63 Year-Old Bachelor   17
Episode   19

II.

The Fall   25
The Mortician   26
Last Dress   27
Grand Emptiness   28
Tracks   29
Wanting   30
Outside There   31
A Funeral   32
A Mercy   33

III.

Eve   37
Permission   39
That's Life   41
Academe   43
Two Cups of Tomatoes   45
For the Sake of Some Sound   47
Young Woman, Living Alone   49
The Middle   50
Blues at 3 AM   51
Nothing Personal   53
Closing   55

IV.

Elk, Washington	59
Where Are We Parked?	61
Catching Up	63
Chivalry	64
The Garden	65
Hysterectomy	66
Getting It Right	67
Early Spring	68

V.

Ode to My Ribcage	73
Zola Lounge, Midnight	75
Laundry	77
The Window	79
Mourning	80
Sentimental	81
Thank You	82
Fiancé	83
Soon It Will Be Time	84

VI.

Teenagers	89
Widow	90
Faith Enough	91
The Simple Exchange	92
Park West Apartments	93
Drive North	95
The Visit	96
Face Down	97
Memorial Day	98

I.

His Yelling

His yelling, a noise
made into music
because I'm listening.
He doesn't know
I'm listening.

He's somewhere
in that empty parking lot—
there aren't enough lights
in this part of town.

And when we're alone
in a parking lot
sometimes we shout
to feel bigger
or smaller.

So he's shouting
for one of those reasons.
"I'm done with drink!"
He says it three times.

I don't say anything,
let him think he's alone.
The silence that follows
is a peace that feels final.

August, Age 24

Standing in front of the open refrigerator,
the light throwing a shadow
of my naked body on the wall.

Water from my just-washed hair
streaks down my back, drops
and pools on the hideous tile.

This is the only cold I could find
on this murky August night.
Through the open window,

I listen to the purr of air conditioners
in other apartments, a train
rumbling in the distance.

To be young is to feel everything
and to want more
than what's in front of you.

Blame

Early morning—
pale light, not yet the stark heat

of midday sun, but something softer.
He spends the early hours

walking through his past,
one eye shut and seeing

everything as it once was,
the other open and squinting

into today's light.
There was a time

when nothing could stop him—
jobs and women came easy,

drugs and drink
kept him skinny,

death was far off.
But the center wouldn't hold.

Soon, not enough work
and too many bills. Soon,

the wife, and then
the ex-wife, the wondering

how love like that
could become such a mess.

Soon, the talk of what's left
in this life—

how many years does he have?
No one can blame him

for asking. But no one
can answer him, either.

He opens both eyes to see
what's in front of him—

the day turning warm,
the cars moving

every which way, the wind
picking things up

and putting them down.
Things are going well for him

now—the subsidized apartment,
the cheap foreign car,

food in the fridge,
a woman to call on the phone

at night—divorced mother
of grown children

who drinks only red wine
and has a laugh like smoke,

rich and thick and fills
up a whole room quick.

No one can blame him
for wanting to forget.

But no one can blame him
for remembering, either.

Unguarded

We were in the kitchen,
he and I, and someone else, too.

    Someone else was talking,

    and we were all ignoring

    the sink stacked with dishes.

He and I stood close but separate,
listening to this someone

say something. He took my hand
without looking at me,

and the music began—
the quiet singing of our bones.

    Someone continued to speak

    of the ordinary.

We stood there, touching,
unguarded.

Honey, I'm Home

Late enough to be dark out,
a time for winding down.

A man in the parking lot, yelling,
"Honey, I'm home," over and over.

This goes on for minutes, minutes more.
I'm at the table with my beer, my book,

listening to this faceless, nameless man,
wondering who he's come home to.

Then the night is quiet again.
I open the door and stare out

into a blackness I can't see.
I hope somebody let him in.

63 Year-Old Bachelor

He's sitting in this diner booth
wearing the same pair of jeans,
the same flannel over shirt
he's had on all week.
He's sitting here, telling us
how he bought a frozen pizza

at the store last night.
This was something he'd never
done before, never cooked
a frozen pizza by himself.
But last night he was excited
about it, he tells us.

Thought of the sticky cheese
on the drive home,
thought of something warm
in his hands. So, he's in
the kitchen, he says, ripping
into the packaging,

and he's ready to cook the thing.
But he realizes he doesn't know
how to turn on the oven.
Stares at it for twenty minutes,
he tells us. Then he thinks
to call his brother,

who's been single

for years. So his brother,
Jon, he comes over.
They figure the oven out.
After, they eat the pizza
on paper plates.

It was just as good
as he expected,
he tells us.

Every damn bite
was good.

Episode

She's inconsolable, kneeling on the linoleum
in that yellow linen dress—same color

as lemon frosting. Her head hangs
from her long neck like a stone,

her face covered by her hands
and tears spilling from her palms.

Her husband, he wants to know why,
he wants to know the cause.

But to her, the cause is meaningless.
What's important is right now,

what's happening now, this
awful collapse, the tightening

of her bones. Truth is,
she dropped the cupcakes.

All 24 of them, in the parking lot
on her way to the fundraiser.

She'd been wearing heels,
not used to their calculating clunk,

and that crack in the asphalt
perfectly placed.

Some of the cupcakes
landed face-down, others

rolled on their sides a ways,
leaving streaks of frosting

across the pavement.
After, she went back inside

to find something, anything else
to bring. And that's when

it happened, this episode,
this revelation of how small,

how silent her life
had become.

II.

The Fall

The cathedral is on fire.
The walls struggle against
an avalanche of flame.

Townspeople gather
in the weed-choked streets
to witness the fall.

The grief is wonderful.
It doesn't matter. The town
has been dead for years.

White skies and white landscape—
it's not easy to live
under such clean light.

The Mortician

I met the mortician at the tavern—
he was three drinks in, talking to the only waitress
about spring and angels.

The top few buttons on the mortician's white shirt
were undone, exposing a pale and hairless chest,
like a lamb shorn for slaughter.

The patrons toasted to their false gods, the ones
enshrined in bottles along the back wall of the bar.
They tossed tragedy down their throats and threw it up

later.

The mortician cried out—he'll drink the sky,
from black to white—he'll drink the dark—
he'll put us all to bed some day.

Last Dress

There will come a time
when someone will decide
how to dress my body
for burial—or rather,

what fabric will burn best
in the furnace,
where I'll be reduced
to a cup of ashes
and some tiny bones.

Even death cannot humble
our unease with nakedness.
But let me remain
uncovered. May my body
be old and sexless,
without attraction or hair.

May my body bear the scars
of love, of childbirth,
of sacrifice. May the skin
pucker and wrinkle
under the weight
of being held
so tightly.

May my last dress
be fire, pure fire,
to carry me blazing
into a lesser place.

Grand Emptiness

Cars without lights idling
alongside the river, watching
the flame of evening spark
and flare before falling
behind the black trees.

After a while, hardly a light
anywhere. We're desperate
for the same, unnamed thing.
Not the moon, but something
like it. Night opens in us

and we drive to wherever it is
we go to rest our heads,
or not rest. Consumed
by the grand emptiness
of living.

Tracks

Darkness is difficult to find
in the city. Many times I turn

my head from the fierce light
of cars coming at me

as I walk alongside the river.
A train whistle carries

through the cold, immediate
yet far away, like the name

of a former lover.
I look to the stars

and find them gone.
The smog is red and heavy.

I keep walking, leaving tracks
in the snow I cannot recognize.

Wanting

This parking lot is the only truth.
We change clothes and names

behind the dumpster. Night falls
at our feet and we are stunned

by the scattering of stars
on the pavement. Dry January—

time of unrealized ambition.
We look up to the cold sky.

"Do you have something more?"

Outside There

Outside there, in the rain,

all is sacred—
                    this is a sacred place,
I can feel it—
                    the disappointments
and the quiet—
                    the wet streets, all the lights
melting together—
                    come back inside
with me now—
                    city of mirrors
and darkness—
                    if I was older
I could say—
                    everything happened
20 years ago—
                    if I was younger
I could say—
                    nothing yet
has happened—
                    I'm stuck here
between past—
                    and the unforeseen
of what's to come—

outside there, in the rain.

A Funeral

Everything's a funeral
at midnight.

The train whistle.
The porch light.

The moon on the windowsill.
The harmonica wailing

through the valley.
The half-sleep murmurs.

The dreams, harvest
of ashes. All of it,

a kind of goodbye.

A Mercy

Everything's a mercy
at sunrise.

The bed kept warm
through the night.

The birds.
The newspaper.

The sear of eggs
in the fry pan.

The cars thrumming
to life, pulling away

from the curb.
All of it,

a kind of hello.

III.

Eve

Sunday, February 15th. 11 AM.
This is not the time
to go to the grocery store

in last night's makeup
and mussed hair. I see myself
in a window before going

inside, and I almost
lose my nerve. I'm wearing
the black overcoat that still

smells like my grandma's
perfume, though she's been
dead a year. The coat

is cinched at the waist
and stops mid-thigh.
And the thighs are the problem—

muscled and bare and red
from the whip of cold.
So much skin is strange

in winter. Beneath
the coat, a white negligee
that doesn't even begin

to cover my ass.
In the foyer, a young girl
hocks cookies

for some fundraiser.
She greets me, and her eyes
fall straight to my legs

and the black stilettos
underneath. This happens
over and over

as I grab the one thing
I need. Finally,
I'm in the check-out line.

And of course, the woman
ahead of me knocks over
the gift card rack, and

of course I stoop down
to help gather the mess,
and of course her kids

must've seen down
or up my coat,
but she said nothing

about it, just thanked me
and stared into my eyes
the whole time.

I leave the store
with a bag of apples
and some new found respect

for girls like me.

Permission

I used to think we all wanted forgiveness.
But what we want is permission
to destroy ourselves, or at least
do a little damage
without feeling guilt or shame.

When we are allowed this,
allowed to control our own pain,
we release our mortality.
We humble ourselves.
We prove imperfection.

The peach on the tree, swollen
with sunlight, wrenched from the branch
and marred with teach,
bruised with greedy hands,
left with only the pit, afterwards.

And don't you think the pit,
shrunken and hard and honest,
is grateful for the loss of flesh
and dappled pageantry,
grateful to be exposed?

Janelle Rainer

That's Life

Your wife left you.
You're between jobs,
and the postman

won't stop bringing bills
to your doorstep.
You spent the last

of your rent money
on bourbon,
and your brother

won't quit asking
for a loan.
The car leaks oil

all over the driveway
like black rain.
You don't feel right

in any of your clothes.
You tell all of this
to someone

who is supposed
to understand.
"That's life."

No, no…

Life is what happens
in those thin hours

between dusk
and dark, between
dawn and day,

when nothing seems
to be going on,
but everything

is right in front
of you.

Academe

Every day there's the drive,
the serious river, the bridge.

Every day there's the hallway,
the rush and blur of bodies,

the sterile classroom. Every day
the white walls, the coffee cup,

the students' handwriting
on notebook paper.

Every day the blouse,
the buttons, the scuffed heels.

Every day the same smiles,
waves, familiar exchange.

Everyday day the sense
of solitude growing deeper.

Every day the simple cry
of living.

Two Cups of Tomatoes

Walking home in the gray light of evening,
watching the working professionals

leave their respective buildings
one by one, watching them ease into their separate cars

and drive away into their separate lives.
I know I am like them, with my pencil skirt,

my buttoned blouse, the manila folder filled
with papers to grade tucked into my leather purse.

Yes, the urban animal.
And I know I am different from them,

because in my hands are two white Styrofoam cups
loaded with cherry tomatoes I picked up

from the market. These cups give me
some color, some mystery, some fire.

I'm walking home and I feel like I have this secret.
Two teenagers are walking toward me, so I cross the street,

not wanting to share. And their cat calls
seem so far away from the fire in my hands

that I hardly notice, don't even look back to sneer.
No, I've got these two cups of tomatoes

and they're still hazy with dust from the garden
and all I'm thinking about is the taste of them,

the release of a long hot summer
as winter comes on.

For the Sake of Some Sound

The rain is persistent.
Lights from the streetlamps and windows
reach far across the wet asphalt
like falling stars, frozen in flight.

Through a break in the clouds,
I find the moon, small
and unsure of itself.

Vehicles glide along
with quiet grace,
and I think of the toy cars
I had as a child,

how I would spin their small wheels
on every surface—
concrete, countertops, the bath tub,

my own legs and arms.
How in love with motion I was,
happy to go anywhere.

And I pray now, thinking
each car outside
must be guided by the hands
of a loving child.

But then I remember the times
when I would smash
two cars together

just for the sake
of some sound.

Young Woman, Living Alone

It's the hour of bare shoulders
and un-bandaged hope, when drinks
are spilled and we make spectacles
of ourselves, dancing in silence.

Some nights I forget to latch the chain
on the front door or to turn
the light off in the kitchen.

At dawn, I find the door
unsecured and I wonder why
no one tried to come for me.

Then I see the kitchen light on
and decide the light kept them away.

The Middle

No more than twenty years old,
and he's in the middle of something.

He explains where he's been
the past three weeks
instead of my English class—

back injury, prescription meds,
pink slip, eviction notice, job search.

He talks in loops, like he's strung out.
I've never seen him without
his straw hat, leather cowboy boots.

Before, he'd sit in the back row,
feet propped on the chair

beside him, dip in his mouth.
He was vocal, and not the type
to raise his hand. Now, he's right

in front of me, without the distance
of a few rows of desks, and I can see

the nail beds of his fingers, ragged
from biting, and I can see the flush of red

around those desperate blue eyes.
And I feel surrounded
by all I cannot do.

Blues at 3 AM

All night long notes
rise up out of
his gut and mix with
the crystallized tune
of the black guitar.

The whole house smells
like the world's oldest hunger—
this need to howl
against the February sky,
this need to answer
all the questions
with song, this need
to know the terror
we are made of.

Our man is hooked
by the chaos
in the cosmos—so deep
that nothing will pull him
back to earth, nothing
but a ghost
dreaming himself
back to flesh.

Nothing Personal

Frazzled lamp posts,
moon hung loosely
in the fog.

Hands and mouths
exchange blessings
with strangers.

What mercy
can you afford
to give me?

My only advice
is to leave,
or to stay.

Most of my decisions
are wrong.
So much of living

is restraint.
Your hands are made
of a great light.

Let's write the oldest
human story
that has nothing

to do with us.
Or everything.
Bodies joined

in blurred prayer
beneath a sky that holds
nothing personal

Closing

I stop work; I shut things down
and turn things off. I step outside

into a night newly born.
My sweater is too thin,

and I feel everything—
the perfect strangeness of the cold.

I start to shiver, so I start
to sing. And the singing

holds the fragrance of a dream—
belonging not to me,

but to this smooth and beautiful evening,
folded in silence.

IV.

Elk, Washington

The Shot Glass smells like cold weather—
the kind of small-town bar

you don't dress up for. Come here
right after work with the pit stains,

the wrinkled shirts, the overalls
with grease smears. Come here

with heavy eyelids, dirty fingernails,
knotted hair. Come here

with stories about a shitty job,
a no-good ex, and a dog that won't stop

howling, because in a bar like this, stories
are just as good as cash.

Tonight, there's a band playing—
older musicians with day jobs,

except for the 22-year-old at the keyboard
with a voice like church and sex

rolled into one—honeysweet soul,
gutbucket blues and gritty rock.

The locals are pulled towards that sound—
swept into the mouth of mo-town songs,

spilling their bodies into each other.
The couple who has been married 20 years

are acting like high-schoolers: she slapping
his chest and arms in a playful girlish way,

he pulling her close and grabbing the flat bones
of her ass. The songs stretch

through midnight, lifting the battered bodies,
bringing them closer to the immensity of the stars

than they've ever been before.

Where Are We Parked?

The cocktail bar is closing
for the night—its neon advertisements
snuffed out, its patrons bloodshot.

Jazz music, fractured barstool stories
and cigarette smoke follow us
out the door. Where are we parked?

Did we go to the old graveyard
among the stones etched in loss,
among the fake flowers?

Did we drive to the distant island, stop
on the wooden bridge varnished
in moonlight?

Did we park out by the harbor
where the ships thrash at their leashes?
Did we decide on a spot beneath

the hulking oaks of spring?
Did we settle in the enlarged shadow
of the white Catholic church on 3rd?

Maybe the car is flushed
with the dense blaze of the streetlamp
in a suburban cul de sac.

Or did we leave it in some forsaken

alley between brick buildings, some city vein
traveled only by lost souls clutching takeout?

The car could be anywhere, outside
an all-night café or behind a barn, even
sunk in some backyard sand box.

Though, now that I think
about it, maybe we walked.
Maybe we flew here.

Catching Up

I will tell you what he told me.
You have me confused
with someone else.

Everything has changed
from what you remember.
Your only option is to leave again.

Remember to say your prayers—
they still count, even if
 you get the words wrong.

The song, the sound of it
will ring true, like the church bell
shattering the night.

Chivalry

Small woman loading heavy boxes
into the trunk of her car.
She doesn't look around.
She doesn't take breaks.
She doesn't brush the sweat
from her forehead. She lifts
with her legs, steady.

But a man comes by anyway
and loads the boxes
two at a time without asking
if she needs help. She thanks him—

she's relieved that the job
is done. Still, she wonders
when we will get tired
of telling this story.

What if she had said no,
cursed him, bit his hands?
Could she bear the look
on his face if she ruined
the world he knows?

The Garden

Morning breaks over the fragile houses.
A low, gray sky.

We spend the day remembering
it was once spring.

The spade rips the haggard grass
from its roots.

He kneels down, lifting handfuls of soil
to his face.

He breathes the damp, the dark.
He smiles at me.

He smiles at this day, happy
to be dirty and sweaty.

We are young like this
for such a short time.

In the turning earth, we hear the groan
of the dead

brought back to life. The day ends
before anyone is ready.

Hysterectomy

Hysterectomy at 26
after giving birth five times.

One more child and you'll die,
the doctor told her.

Not like when people say
one more bite of food

and I'll die, or
one more meeting

and I'll die. No, this
was 1956. Things

were more serious then.
So a part of her

was removed, and she
went on being

a wife, a mother,
and I wonder

if she ever felt ruined
in some small way,

or if she was too full
of other things

to even notice
something missing.

66   Janelle Rainer

Getting It Right

"I'm pushing as hard as I can," the girl says.

Nine or ten years old, maybe. Pink bike,
pink leggings, pink jacket. She's almost

made it to the top of the hill, where the pavement
flattens. Her brother, younger, rides ahead.

Behind, a man wearing khakis
and a plaid shirt, barely pedaling.
The sun lights up his gray hair.

"You're doing fine," he says,
then corrects himself.

"You're doing great, actually."

Early Spring

When the sun is out, I'm never ready
to go inside. That's why I'm on this bench,

sitting cross-legged to watch the light fall
steadily into evening. It may be forty degrees

and the wind may be tossing my hair around
like a cold, careless lover, but I can't

just let the sun go, not yet. It deserves
the same kind of goodbye a mother gives

her child—the familiar hug and kiss
of parting bodies, and the mother watching

and waving until the child
is out of sight.

V.

Ode to My Ribcage

My fingers glaze over
the scaffolding
inside my chest

as I dress in the morning.
I imagine a collection
of moon-white branches,

perfectly arranged.
Each slender, stubborn bone
is a beautiful stranger.

Reminders of the raw story
beneath my skin.
Lungs flare and fade.

My heart hangs
like a lopsided sun.
Some day my body will fail

and these hooked wings
will crank open, revealing
a scalding light.

Zola Lounge, Midnight

"Whatever my eyes desired I did not keep from them;
I kept my heart from no pleasure."

–Ecclesiastes

The Samoan singer croons
of love, her voice deep and blurred
among the clink
of half-full glasses,
trembling hands toasting
to time, the drift of sun
and sleep.

Outside, smokers lean
against the brick wall.
Gray mist lifts
towards the white stars,
swollen moon.

People of long ago
are forgotten,
and people yet to come
are not promised.
There is a season
for everything, and this
is our time.

Follow the desires
of your eyes—may we all
slide into one another

like melting ice as we dance
on knotted floor planks.

May we all fall in love
with the tilt of a stranger's head
before we scatter
into the night,
before the dust of our dreams
returns to earth.

Laundry

In the apartment below, voices
rise and fall like the tide—

white-capped anger and ebbs
of sorrow-laced silence.

Only a matter of time before
the door will crack shut

and the man will yellow under
the streetlamp outside, cigarette

smoke threading from his grimace
as he begs the stars to come closer.

Yes, I see him now, a weedy figure
pacing the streetlamp's haze

on the sidewalk. I always expect him
to grip a battered suitcase in his hand,

to be all set to search elsewhere
for happiness, but so far he stays

and smokes. I hear the woman
scrubbing dishes below, porcelain

clanking in the suds, water
rushing from the faucet.

I hear their washing machine enter
its spin cycle, whirling violently

as if it's close to take-off, then quieting,
then shutting down altogether.

The Window

I looked back
and I could see him
through the window,

standing in the kitchen,
his hands in his pockets,

his red sweater
made more red
by the white walls.

Mourning

"Yes, I understand that I'm to set you free."
                                    –Patsy Cline

Two weeks ago, I cut
my left ring finger while
slicing strawberries.

I cried out in shock, not
pain. The pain came
after. But there was something
miraculous about it—

the inward flowing
outward, going somewhere
uncharted, a kind of trespass.

Now, the wound tears open
every couple of days—
refusing to heal.

Sentimental

Another lease finished.
People leave, and the house
seems bigger or smaller without them—
just as a past lover is remembered
for being full of light,
or full of darkness, but rarely
full of both, as we all are.

Thank You

Is there a place they go
inside of themselves,
inside of each other,

when the night is eaten
by birdsong
and the sun lifts higher,
sheer as a paper umbrella?

A new day seems impossible
considering the relentless perfection
of yesterday.

The sand beneath their feet,
the sunset, the sparks of song
rising into the night,
the fusion,

the simple straw hat.
She forgot to say thank you
before falling asleep,

but he knows.

Fiancé

I needed apples, so I walked to the store
as the sun was falling.

Inside, the white lights felt like snow
on my eyes, too cold and bright.

Inside, a large wooden crate
filled with pumpkins.

I felt the rough stem of a round one
near the top, and imagined us

sitting cross-legged in a kitchen
someday, somewhere,

carving pumpkins, our hands
shining with the muck.

This imagined moment was so ordinary,
so domestic.

And I realized if we carved pumpkins,
if we did this simple thing

together, year after year,
we'll make it.

The simple acts
will save us.

Soon It Will Be Time

The day closes up outside, quietly as it began.
A few strung-out clouds move away from the setting
sun.

Soon it will be time for the cool apple,
the handful of almonds, the haloed light over the table.

Soon it will be time for the robe with no sash,
the strip of tight skin where it opens.

Soon it will be time for the transparent darkness,
the stars in the window.

"Nothing could be simpler," she says.
She knows he's alive, and she owns that.

She reads Gabriel Garcia Marquez
and grows more suited for love.

VI.

Teenagers

The gas station attendant—
she must've thought we were teenagers,
a little too wide-eyed and disheveled
for adult life.

Me, with my raccoon eyes
and barely-there frayed shorts—
you, with bits of grass stuck in your hair
from the daytime loungings.

She must've thought we were escaping,
running away together in a frenzy
of hormones and rebellion,
bringing only the clothes on our backs (such as they were).

She must've thought we would try
to weasel some booze out of her,
flirt just enough that she wouldn't ID us
but wouldn't get the wrong impression, either.

She must've thought she'd get noise complaints
from the rooms next to ours,
so she was smart about it,
put us almost at the end.

She must've thought we were ghosts
from her past—gauzy and ageless—
impossibly cruel, perfect.

Widow

The black-and-white river of winter
cuts through the valley,

flows beneath the bridge he built
forty years ago.

"We never see such high waters
in December," he says. "Very unusual."

He still speaks in plural,
though she's been gone a full year.

I picture him in the early hours
of morning, momentarily confused

by the emptiness beside him
before he's full awake,

and remembers.

Faith Enough

The man is asleep on the couch.
In front of him, a sitcom plays
on the screen with the sound off.

A woman sits beside him, awake,
facing his defenseless quiet
to see him the way

his birth mother found him
in her arms, sleeping
for the first time, small

and in need of mercy
and warmth. She imagines
the sighs of his parents

when they found him
asleep in his door-less room,
the stillness so different

from his wakeful scheming.
We sleep, and we are young
again. We sleep, and we trust

the wakeful to watch
over us, to guide us through
from one world to the next.

I'm here, she says.
He doesn't move.
His stillness is faith enough.

The Simple Exchange

The storybooks of our childhood
built bridges to somewhere
that was not adulthood.

Now, he is old and singing
of his young voice.
And she is old, painting herself

as she once was, those small curves
that used to be hers. Now, they're old.
In bed, their bones get all tangled,

like tree branches in the wind.
They've returned to what was
beneath the beauty—

the simple exchange of putting each other
back together every morning.
This loving without a need

for the immortal.

Park West Apartments

The girl from 207, she's sprawled flat on her back
under the maple tree, an open book resting on her face.

The woman in 108 steps outside for no more than a few seconds,
then retreats, red door shutting slowly.

205 is home on his lunch break, smoking on the balcony
in his grease-stained mechanic clothes.

105 leaves before sun-up and returns at dusk,
limping across the courtyard in his peculiar gait.

A man with a small child climbs the concrete stairs
to knock on 208, where the tweakers live.

Such a strange calm in this midday heat,
just a day from October.

It's as if time himself has taken an afternoon nap,
and woke up stunned, exhausted, unsure of himself

and unable to leave his dreams behind.
106, the veteran with the bird feeder outside his door,

walks through the grass to stand above 207,
says something to her in his South Carolina accent.

She moves for the first time in a long while,
lifting the book from her face with her hand.

She says something back, in a voice too high
for his age-numbed ears, but she's smiling,

so he smiles, too. They talk without words
for a moment, then wave goodbye to each other,

ghosts of their own history.

Drive North

Tired of mankind on a Friday—
we drive North. The landscape

shifts from box stores
to suburban estates,

then from residential to rural,
from farms to forests of pine.

The lift and fall of the road
along the river.

We stay quiet and contemplate
fulfillment. We think about

our choices. The road splits
from the river. We find

the junkyards of happy poverty.
We ask what it means

to stop wanting.

The Visit

The side door is always unlocked,
so I let myself in.

He was reading in the chair
by the window, still wearing
his leather work boots.

Took off my coat, my gloves,
stayed quiet. He didn't' startle.

Must be a good book, I thought.
I sat down in the chair
beside him. Noticed his eyes

were closed. Breathing…
couldn't tell. I got up

and stood by his side.
Touched his bony shoulder.
His eyes fluttered, thank God,

and he looked at my hand.
The hand on his shoulder.

A hand that could belong
to anybody. Then he looked
up, to my face. A face

that could belong to anybody.
"Where did you come from?"

Face Down

When I was a child
there was an old man
who died on the corner
of a very busy street
face down on the pavement.
I stopped sleeping for days
because I slept face down.
I wasn't ready to die.
That's how the mind works
when we are so young.
If it happened to you
it will happen to me.
Now, my mind is older.
Now, my heart is fierce.
But fear stays the same.
Fear is the dark, nothing.
Fear is the light, blind.
A phone rings all day
and no one will answer.

Memorial Day

I laid down because
it was a warm day

and the sun on my face
felt like an answered prayer.

I laid down because
the yellowed rectangle of grass

didn't seem like enough
to keep you covered.

I laid down because
the world felt so heavy.

I laid down to listen
to the wind, the birds.

I laid down to feel
closer to you.

I laid down because
I didn't know how else

to name my grief.
I laid down because

I love you
and I miss you.

I laid down because
I wasn't ready to leave.

Acknowledgments

Atticus Review: "63 Year-Old Bachelor"

ATOMIC: "The Fall"

Cacti Fur: "Chivalry"

Emerge Literary Journal: "Permission"

Harpur Palate: "Ode to My Ribcage"

The Rain, Party, & Disaster Society: "Drive North"

Made in the USA
Middletown, DE
19 April 2016